THE WAYS OF GOD IN GRACE

illustrated by

THE WAYS OF GOD IN CREATION

By E W Bullinger

ISBN: 978-1-78364-556-5

www.obt.org.uk

****

THE OPEN BIBLE TRUST
Fordland Mount, Upper Basildon,
Reading, RG8 8LU, UK

THE WAYS OF GOD IN GRACE

illustrated by

THE WAYS OF GOD IN CREATION

Contents

INTRODUCTION

INTRODUCTION

Our subject in this Bible study is,

**The ways of God in grace
illustrated by the ways of God in creation.**

In the first chapter of Genesis we have the record of what we may call the old creation, because in the fifth chapter of the second epistle to the Corinthians it is linked with the new creation. "If any man be in Christ, he is a new creature" – *i.e.* a new creation (R.V., margin), *i.e.* a new created thing.

> "Old things are passed away; behold, all things are become new. And all things are of God."

When we have the word "behold" as we have here – "behold, all things are become new" – we may look upon it as emphatically the word of the Holy Ghost; not a mere interjection, but a command telling us to behold, to see, to note, to observe; just as we may look on "Verily" as peculiarly the word of Christ – "Verily, verily, I say unto you"; and as we may regard the word "Yea" as peculiarly associated with the Father. (2 Cor. 1:20).

But, passing on, let us first of all define our term – the word "grace." We all know that its simple meaning is *favour*; but what kind of favour is it?

- We show favour to the poor and we call it *pity*.
- We show favour to the sorrowful and the suffering, and we call it *compassion*.
- Favour is shown to the miserable and we call it *mercy*.

- Favour is shown to the obstinate, and perverse, and rebellious, and we call it *patience*.

But grace is favour shown to the *unworthy*, because it is shown to those who not only do not deserve it, but who deserve the very opposite.

> Grace is the favour of God when there is nothing to draw it forth, nothing to elicit it any way – the uninfluenced favour of God – and in this view creation was at any rate in a sense a work of grace.

That is to say, there was no reason why God should create; so far as we know, of course, or are told. There was no necessity upon His part, for "all things are of God." It is just the same in the new creation.

But man's effort has ever been, and is, to shut God out; and just as he has invented his theories of evolution to shut God out of creation, so man has used "free-will" to shut God out of His work of grace in the conversion of the sinner. Man regards both as a mere development – as an improvement of something already existing. But God declares that in both creations His work is something altogether new. And notice in this record of creation (Gen. 1:1-2:3) how effectually God seems to have anticipated man's theory, and how He has effectually shut it out. Instead of one thing being evolved or developed from another, we see everywhere a divine and glorious person, moving, acting and speaking.

Thirty-five times we have the word "God" (seven times five, that is the perfection of grace). If five be the number of grace, as it is, then we have the perfection of God's ways in grace. The pronouns, of course we have oftener.

But connected with the name of God in this record we have ten words, and thirty-five times these ten words are used:

- "God created,"
- "God moved,"
- "God said,"
- "God saw,"
- "God divided,"
- "God called,"
- "God made,"
- "God set,"
- "God blessed,"
- "God ended."

In order to shut out forever all man's theories and speculations as to creation, God has introduced *Himself*, and we see God Himself at every movement and at every turn, the great divine Creator.

Four of these words are used only *once*:

- "moved,"
- "divided,"
- "set,"
- "ended"

But the word "blessed" does not occur until the fifth day – not until there is life, or a living, moving creature.

- Five times we have the word "created,"
- seven times the word "saw," and

- ten times the word "said."

With what reverence should we approach this scene. With what reverence should we listen to the utterances of the Creator about His own work, so that we may say with David, not only,

"Thy word is true from the beginning,"

but as it is in the margin also (and I believe that many of these duplicate readings are not that we should shut out one and take in the other, but there is a sense in which they are both correct).

"The beginning of thy word is true."

There are two books of the Bible against which Satan has shown the greatest possible enmity. One of them is the book of Genesis, and the other is the Apocalypse.

- The first book tells us of grace begun, and the last of grace ended in glory.
- The first book tells of Satan's curse, and the last of Satan's doom.

No wonder then that he vents his greatest enmity against these two books.

Let us, then, approach this perfect record of God's work, the record of Him who performed it, and we shall see what was in the mind of the Creator at that moment concerning the work of grace in the heart of every saved sinner.

THE
FIRST DAY

THE FIRST DAY

And, first, with regard to "the beginning."

The beginning of God's creation was good and perfect. The very word "created" implies that. It means to cut or carve or to polish. The familiar word for creation is "*cosmos*," and that is frequently translated "ornament" (Exod. 33:5; Isa. 49:18; Jer. 4:30). In the epistle of Peter, speaking of holy women, we have the expression "whose adorning." (*Cosmos* is here translated "adorning," 1 Peter 3:3). Everything that could give us the idea of perfection and beauty and order is implied in this first verse.

But then you come to the second verse, and you read that "the earth was without form and void."

The word "was" (*hayah*) is the common term for "it came to pass." It is not the mere verb "to be." *Hayah*, rendered "and it came to pass," "it came to pass," "it came to pass," occurs again and again in this very record (see, for example, Gen. 4:3, 8; 6:1; 7:10; 8:6 etc.) It came to pass then, in some way and at some time, and for some reason which is not revealed, that the earth became "*tohoo*." That is the word that is translated here "without form." It was not created so, it became so.

And here there is no question as to the meaning of words – no hair splitting between lexicographers or wresting of scripture to suit the successive theories of science so called; but we have what God Himself tells us in a very important scripture, Isa. 45:18. Here you have the Creator speaking.

"Thus saith the Lord that created the heavens; God Himself that formed the earth and made it."

(And He ought to know how He made it, and why He made it. He ought to be able to speak on this wonderful subject, and He says),

"He hath established it, He created it not in vain."

i.e., "Not *tohoo*." Here the same word (*tohoo*) is translated "in vain." In Genesis it is rendered "without form"; but never mind what it really means for the moment. Whatever it means, the great fact is that it was *not created so*. The Creator distinctly informs us that "He created it not *tohoo*"; and therefore you have the irresistible conclusion that, as I have said, in some way and at some time and for some reason which is not revealed, *it became tohoo*; it became empty, waste, desolate – it became a ruin. Thus we have, with regard to the old creation, first, a scene of perfection, and then a scene of ruin.

You have just the same with man. You have the same with Adam. Man also was created upright and perfect and in the image of God; but he became a ruin. We are not told when. We know not *how long* he continued in this state of perfection; and we are not told *why* he became a ruin; but we *are told* in this case *how*. We are not even told *how* with regard to the old creation, but we *are* told how man became a ruin. You have the record of it in chapter 3. There is the history of the ruin.

In Eccl. 7:29 it says, "God hath made man upright; but they have sought out many inventions." "Thou hast destroyed thyself" (Hosea 13:9). "This is the judgment of God." Empty, waste, desolate.

The ruin is described in Eph. 2:1, 2, in words which are familiar to you, such a ruin that men are described as "dead in trespasses and sins," "lying in the wicked one," "children of wrath." In Titus 3:1-3 you have another description of this ruin.

But this is not our point. Our point is not the ways of man in ruin, but the ways of God in grace, delivering from the ruin.

Now go back to the old creation, and where did the change, the re-creation, begin? You have it in the Gen 1:2, "The Spirit of God moved." It was not from the working of any laws, then; not from any evolution or development; but "the Spirit of God moved." That is where the old creation began, and that also is where the new creation begins. The Spirit of God *moves* in your heart and mine, and that is the beginning of our re-creation. "Not of blood, nor of the will of the flesh, nor of the will of man, but of God." (John 1:13). "Old things are passed away, (2 Cor. 5:17).

What is the next step? "And God said."

The "word" of God then was the next thing. "And God said." These were the two agencies in the old creation - first "the Spirit of God," then "the word of God." These are the two agencies in the new creation also, for we are said to be "born of the SPIRIT," and born also of the WORD. "So is every one that is born of the Spirit" is the proof of the one (John 3:8), and 1 Peter 1:23 is the proof of the other,

> "Being born again, not of corruptible seed, but of incorruptible, by the word of God, which liveth and abideth for ever."

This then is the order in both creations. First, God moves, *i.e.* "the Spirit of God." Then God speaks.

What is the next thing? LIGHT.

"The entrance of Thy words giveth light." (Psa. 119:130). What is the next thing? What does the light shine on? It shines on the ruin. There is nothing else for it to shine on. It shines upon the desolation: and when the Spirit of God has moved in our hearts, and His word has spoken to our souls, and light has entered, it shines on the ruin and reveals to us our lost condition. Thus the first effect of the light is sorrow, trouble, anxiety, and distress – in other words, conviction of sin. This is the origin of repentance. This is the source of conversion.

It is not some frame of mind into which you can work yourselves, as the Jesuits do, by contemplating for a week a certain number of subjects or pictures. It is not from "the will of the flesh, nor the will of man, but it is of God." This, I say, is the origin of repentance. Any other source of what looks like conversion is only fictitious, and it is surprising to what a high religious condition the flesh can be wrought up. Ravishing music, pathetic anecdotes, persuasive appeals, can easily produce sensations in the flesh. But there is nothing in them. They will not last. They fade away like the morning cloud or like the early dew. There is all too much of this in the present day, and that is why there is so much disappointment amongst Christian workers.

There is so much excitement accompanying the preaching of the gospel that it is difficult to tell where one begins and the other ends. It is difficult to see what is the result of excitement and what is the work of the Spirit. Anything that looks like life, any work apparently spiritual work, which does not commence with conviction of sin and with sorrow for sin, is not produced by the Spirit of God moving, or by the word of God speaking. There is nothing true in it; nothing really good, and nothing permanent.

And yet on every hand today sinners are exhorted to "believe." This is the first thing which they are told to do, quite apart from any evidence of conviction of sin, or of sorrow for sin, or of any movement of the Spirit of God. What is the result? The Lord Himself has told us in Mark 4:16, 17:

> "These are they likewise which are sown on stony ground; who, when they have heard the word, IMMEDIATELY receive it with gladness; and have no root in themselves, and so endure but for a time: afterward, when affliction or persecution ariseth for the Word's sake, IMMEDIATELY they are offended."

The one is just as "immediate as the other. Therefore, Christian workers, beware of this "gladness," because the divine result of the Spirit of God moving and the word of God speaking and of the light shining upon the ruin, will never be "gladness" at first. The gladness comes afterwards, but not at the first.

This, then, is the divine order. The words of Paul to the Philippian jailer are often quoted to persons who are not in the jailer's condition:

> "Believe on the Lord Jesus Christ, and thou shalt be saved."

God has joined faith with repentance, and what God hath joined together no man can put asunder without marring the truth. "Repentance and faith" is God's order; and we may say, without hesitation, that there was conviction of sin in the heart of that jailer. You remember the scene. He was in prison: it was quite dark. He took a sword, and was going to slay himself, knowing that he should have an ignominious death in the morning (Acts 12:19), and therefore he would rather put himself to death.

"He drew out his sword, and would have killed himself, supposing that the prisoners had been fled." (Acts 16:27)

Now, picture the scene in the darkness of that night. There is the man with a sword in his hand, and with these thoughts in his mind. He hears a voice from the inner prison saying:

"Do thyself no harm."

Then there is an eye which can see him in that darkness; and knows what he is about to do!

"We are all here."

Then there is someone who knows what he is thinking about! That man saw himself in the presence of God, and conviction was wrought in his mind. The Spirit of God had moved, and the word of God had spoken through His servant. No wonder he asked:

"What must I do to be saved?"

And anyone who asks that question has seen himself as a lost sinner, and felt his need of the Saviour.

No, the effect of the light at first is not pleasant, because it only reveals to us what we are. Nevertheless, it is written:

"God saw the light that it was good."

Thank God, then, for the light! Let us not be occupied with what the light shines upon, but let us rather look up and thank God for the light, and for the evidence that, "He has begun a good work," even a new creation, which He will never leave till He has finished it (Phil. 1:6).

This is the source of all true anxiety for sin. There was a man about whom I had been anxious for some time, and one day he came and told me that he was very anxious about his soul. I said:

> "Thank God; now I am not anxious. I have been anxious about you for a long time, but I need not be anxious any longer."

Why? Because his anxiety was the evidence that the Spirit of God had moved; that the word of God had spoken to him, and I knew therefore whence his anxiety about his soul had come, and that God would finish the work He had begun.

It is not only thus the beginning of the new creation, but it is the same ever afterwards with regard to our growth in grace. The more light we have – the more of this blessed light which comes through the Spirit of God and the word of God – the more shall we discern the depth of our ruin, and the more shall we be dissatisfied with ourselves.

Some of you may have known what it is to have slept a sound sleep in a strange room. You awake in the darkness of night, but you cannot discern a single object in the darkness. That is our condition by nature, "dead in trespasses and sins" – not seeing or knowing such a thing as sin in our experience.

But presently, as we lie awake, a glimmer of light comes, and we see one dark object here, and another dark object there; but we cannot tell what any object is, whether it is a door or any article of furniture. A little more light comes, and we begin to distinguish what the objects in the room are; and presently, when the sunlight streams in, we see every speck of dust, every spot, every stain.

And it will be so with us as God gives us more and more of His light. As we "walk in the light" the more we shall see of ourselves, the more we shall see that certain things are sinful now which, a year ago, we thought not to be sinful. That is why you see sin where you never saw it before, and the more light you have the more you will be dissatisfied with yourselves. Nevertheless, thank God for the light.

"God saw the light that it was good."

Now the solemn question is, where are we with reference to these things? Do we know anything of these experiences? Has the true light shone into our hearts? This is no mere fanciful theory; for the Spirit of God has Himself linked them together.

"For God, who commanded the light to shine out of darkness, hath shined in our hearts, to *give* the light of the knowledge of the glory of God in the face of Jesus Christ." (2 Cor. 4:6)

So we have here, on the first day, the first work, the first giving of divine light, and the result of that light, by which we first discovered our ruined condition, and by which also we learn to see God in the face of Jesus Christ. Let us "walk in the light!"

Walking in the light reveals to us, as nothing else can do, the "iniquity of our holy things." It is most noteworthy that in 1 John 1:7 the mention of the blood is introduced in connection with walking in the light. This is not where man would have mentioned it.

When man talks of walking in the light he does not mention the blood. The Spirit of God brings in the blood when He says,

"Walk in the light, as He is in the light . . . and the blood of Jesus Christ His Son cleanseth us from all sin." (1 John 1:7)

Than is the moment at which we have need to be reminded of the gracious cleansing power of the blood – when the divine light in which we walk reveals to us the iniquity of our holy things. Strange to say, in the first verse 1 John 2, where it says, "If any man sin," there is no reference to the blood! But that is just the place where man would have brought it in if this had been man's book.

"If any man sin, we have an advocate with the Father."

There is no reference to the blood. But we are reminded that our relationship has not been broken by sin. God is still our Father.

"If any man sin, we have an advocate with the Father, Jesus Christ the righteous."

THE
SECOND DAY

THE SECOND DAY

Now we come to the second day.

In the second day only a firmament was created. It was really a work of separation; it was a dividing work. And the second day is like the second of the life-type of Genesis; Cain and Abel.

Jukes, and others, have pointed out the very types in the books are all in harmony with the subject and teaching of those books. For example,

- Exodus is the book of *redemption*, and its types are types of redemption.
- Numbers is the book of the *wilderness*, and its types are wilderness types.
- Leviticus is the book of *worship*, and its types are types of worship.
- But Genesis is the book of *life*, and its types are lives – seven lives.

Adam is the life that illustrates the first day – the ruined sinner quickened by grace.

The life that illustrates the second day is a double one – Cain and Abel. In the midst of the ruin and the confusion, that is come to the life below, a new nature has been implanted – a new nature that can never mingle with the old nature, for the old nature is never changed into the new.

"That which is born of the flesh is flesh, and that which is born of the Spirit is spirit." (John 3:8)

There is no known process by which the flesh can be converted into spirit. You may train it and educate it as you please, or improve it or cultivate it as you will, but it is still "flesh." It is only improved flesh. It is not spirit, for only "that which is born of the Spirit is spirit."

On this second day there was merely the firmament made to divide that which was above from that which was below; which in the new creation is the separation of the two natures. And so the first result of the divine life in the soul is the learning of the existence of the two natures. This second day is the only day that is not called "good." There was no solid ground out of which any fruit could be produced; there was only that which divided heavenly from earthly things.

But when we come to …

THE THIRD DAY

THE THIRD DAY

We have a great day! It is a double-day, divided into two parts.

The number three speaks of resurrection. The Lord rose from the dead upon the third day. And the number three is always stamped as a resurrection number. It answers to the third life-type in this book of Genesis. Noah was the man who stood upon a new earth, a type of the new resurrection life in the soul.

And what was the work of the first part of this day? It was the gathering of the waters together and calling them seas; and the raising up of the dry land out of the waters.

> "Thou hast set a bound that they may not pass over; that they turn not again to cover the earth." (Psa. 104:9).

That is the order of God's work in the old creation; and that is the next stage of His work in the new. Our old nature receives bounds like these waters, and the dry land appears – that new nature out of which God can produce fruit. "Quickened with Christ" is the truth of the first and second days. "Risen with Christ" is the truth of the third day. This is Romans 8. Dead with Christ and risen with Christ. That is where grace puts us in the new creation. "If any man be in Christ." It does not say, "If any man be born again," or, "If any man be converted"; but, "If any man be IN CHRIST." Then, and then only, "old things are passed away: behold, all things have become new."

It is not a question here of what is *in us*. It is not a question of what is produced from us. It is not a question here of what is experienced by us; but the question is, "If any man be in Christ."

Everything depends upon that. As I said, the waters are "gathered," and they are bounded; but they are not removed: they are not taken away. You might as easily take away the flesh from your nature, as take away the waters from off the face of the earth. The flesh is in us, but, thank God, we are "not in the flesh" any more (Rom. 8:9). We are in Christ; and all who are in Christ are in the new creation, on resurrection ground.

I have said that this third day was a great day. It has two parts. Twice on this day we have the words, "God said"; and twice you have the formula, "God saw that it was good."

In the first half of this day He raises up the earth from out from the waters, and in the second half of the day He produces fruit from it.

> "Being now made free from sin, and become servants to God, we have our fruit unto holiness." (Romans 6:22)

And it is God who produces the fruit. This is the testimony of Eph. 2:10:

> "For we are His workmanship, created in Christ Jesus unto good works, which God hath before ordained that we should walk in them."

"Good works" are therefore of God's creation. They are works produced by His Spirit, which God hath before ordained" (margin, "*prepared*") "that we should walk in them."

There are three kinds of "works" described in the Word of God.

- There are "wicked works" which are the "works of the flesh."
- There are "dead works" which are also produced from the flesh; they look like "good works" in outward appearance, but they are not the "fruit of the Spirit," and are therefore "dead." They appear to be like "good works," but not being produced by the Spirit of God, and not coming from faith in God, "they have the nature of sin." (Article 13; Rom. 14:23).
- Then there are "good works" which are the products of that new nature implanted in us by God – works which God has "prepared for us to walk in," and which He has produced in us. "Fruit unto holiness" can be produced only from the risen life, the life of God imparted to us in the new nature.

> "God called the dry land earth."

The most probable root of the word "earth" has reference to something *solid* and *firm*, as opposed to the waters, which are not so. It is only out of that new nature which God has "strengthened, established, and settled" that these fruits can be produced.

> "I can do all things through Christ which strengtheneth me." (Phil. 4:13)

And this fruit is, you will observe, from the tender "grass" to the "fruit tree," whose seed is in itself. The definition of fruit is that which contains the seed. This new divine life implanted in us contains its seed within itself; that seed produces the fruit, and that fruit again contains its own seed.

Moreover, the fruit is for the Master's use. The fruit is not for the use of the tree. The fruit is for the use and the pleasure of the one who owns the tree. "Herein," said the Lord Jesus Christ, in John 15:8, "is My Father glorified, that ye bear much fruit." It is for the glory of the Father therefore that the fruit is to be produced.

Further, notice the way in which the fruit is produced. The tree does not try to produce it. There is no effort on the part of the tree. All that the tree has to do is to lift up its head to heaven, to drink in heaven's air and water, and heaven's light, and the fruit will come without effort. "We beholding" – and beholding – and beholding – there is no restless effort on our part, no anxious toiling to be this, or do that, or to produce the other. But it is,

> "We beholding . . . *are changed* into the same image." (2 Cor. 3:18)

There is the fruit.

A beautiful illustration, and a solemn lesson, is afforded by the following facts, which form a true parable. A well-known nursery gardener, near London, always knew, when he was a boy, where to take his companions to find the best fruit in his father's grounds. When he became a man, and the business became his own, he asked himself how it was that he always found the best fruit in that particular place.

> "Could it be on account of the situation? No. Was it on account of the aspect or the light? No. Or was it through anything in the soil? No."

There was nothing; and at last he concluded that it must be *because the trees had been moved there.* They were trees that had been transplanted. He thus discovered the great principle of *root-*

pruning in order to make the trees produce fruit. Every third or fourth year this principle is to dig round the tree and prune the long lateral roots. That is the great secret. We leave a fruit tree a long time in the ground; the roots spread out; they go deep into the earth; they make a fine tree, a fine show – plenty of leaves; but *there is no fruit*! The roots have never been pruned. There is plenty of blossom, but we are disappointed again and again to find no fruit. Herein is a parable!

It is exactly so with ourselves: we put forth blossom and leaves; we make a fine show, but there is no fruit for the Master's use, because our roots have not been pruned. That is what we need, and our Heavenly Gardener knows how to prune our roots: He knows how to prevent them from going too deeply into the earth. Many a divine intervention is used for that purpose, many a discipline, but the result is "fruit unto God."

God's children know something of what this root-pruning is. It is not a pleasant process at the time; for:

> "No chastening for the present seemeth to be joyous, but grievous: nevertheless afterward it yieldeth the peaceable fruit of righteousness unto them which are exercised thereby." (Heb. 12:11)

We come now to …

THE
FOURTH DAY

THE FOURTH DAY

This introduces us to a heavenly scene. Sun, moon, and stars are created.

If the work of the first and second day is expressed by the words "quickened with Christ," and if the work of the third day is "risen with Christ," then this fourth day is "seated in the heavenlies with Christ," for it is a heavenly scene.

The fourth life-type of Genesis is Abraham, and in him we see the manifestation of this divine life in the world and before men – a life that was in the world, not of it. It was a life of faith. Abraham was a man who was characterized by separation from the world. He went out from the world "a stranger and a pilgrim" (not a pilgrim and a stranger, for we must be strangers to the world before we can be pilgrims in it). He walked before God. It was the manifestation of this heavenly life in his earthly walk before men.

Now what is the teaching of the sun, moon, and stars? You have it is Psa. 89:36, 37:

> "His seed shall endure for ever, and his throne as the sun before Me. It shall be established for ever as the moon, and as a FAITHFUL WITNESS in heaven."

These heavenly bodies are God's *witnesses*. Who was "the faithful witness"? The Lord Jesus. Only of Him could it be said that He was a "faithful witness." (Rev. 1:5). We are witnesses only in part – witnesses according to our measure.

The "moon" we take to illustrate the saints *collectively* in the Church, and the "stars" the saints *individually*. What is their function? It says here that they are to "give light upon the earth." That is the work of the moon and of the stars? And is not that the function of the Church, and of the individual members of it, to "give light upon the earth" during the absence of Jesus their Lord, "the Sun of Righteousness," who is now absent from the earth? This world is a "dark place" (2 Pet. 1:19). Now it is night. But, thank God, the same Scripture that tells us that it is night tells us that "the night is far spent." (Rom. 13:12). It tells us also that "the day is at hand," that a glorious day is coming, when the sun and moon shall shine together, when the "sun shall no more go down; neither shall the moon withdraw itself" (Isa. 60:20).

The moon and stars now do not *always* give their light upon the earth. There are many nights that are very dark. The moon also is characterized by its perpetual changes. It is only a short time at the full. And the stars are often hidden. So it is with our testimony.

But as there is a day coming when the sun shall no more go down, and the moon shall not withdraw herself, so there is a day soon to dawn when we shall be with Christ. There will be no more change then; no more failures in manifestation; for

> "When Christ who is our life shall appear, then shall we also appear with Him in glory." (Col. 3:4)

Let us meanwhile remember for our comfort the word that is written:

> "He telleth the number of the stars; He calleth them all by their names." (Psa. 147:4)

They may differ in glory, just as His sheep may differ in their characteristics; but

"He calleth the sheep by name" (John 10:3).

Yes, His own sheep are *numbered* and *named*.

Now we come to …

THE
FIFTH DAY

THE FIFTH DAY

We have a change, a great change.

The break is marked by the word "create," which we have not had since the first verse. The number seven is always divided into four and three; we have had the four days, and now we have the three. We cannot get any higher than in heavenly places in Christ. As we cannot get higher, we must come back to an earthly scene to realise our *blessing* in the world by experience. On this fifth day we have the words "God blessed" for the first time.

We come back from the heavenly to an earthly scene. On this day is created "the moving creature that hath life." This answers to this new creation life, living and moving in the world, as it does also to the fifth life-type which is Isaac. It is the blessing of "sonship" known in the earth, and the chastening of sons too, which always accompanies sonship (Heb. 12:11).

The waters represent disquietude; never resting, casting up mire and dirt, sorrow and suffering; but they are all made to minister blessing, because there is blessing pronounced for the first time on this fifth day. "Nevertheless afterward" (Heb. 12:11).

> "If children, then heirs; heirs of God, and joint heirs with Christ; if so be that we suffer with *Him*, that we may be also glorified together." (Rom. 8:17)

God brings forth this blessing out of the waters, out of the sorrow and the suffering of this present life. After having realized our position and our security "in Christ," we have to learn our state, and to live this life in a world of disquietude.

We have to live with the flesh in us, and there is nothing in all these waters for the sustenance of this new spiritual life. We experience the power of "the will of the flesh," and we need the experience if, out of the waters of affliction, "the peaceable fruit of righteousness" is to be yielded. (Heb. 12:11). Hence we are enabled to "glory also in tribulations" (Rom. 5:3). Thus is *blessing* brought out of the waters of trial and tribulation.

We may take the life-type of Jacob with this fifth day. For, while in Isaac we have the *adoption* of sons, in Jacob we have the *discipline* of sons. In fact, 2 Cor. 4:15-18 is the passage which sums up the teaching of the fifth day's work:

> "All things *are* for your sakes, that the abundant grace might through the thanksgiving of many rebound to the glory of God. For which cause we faint not; but through our outward man perish, yet the inward *man* is renewed day by day. For our light affliction, which is but for a moment, worketh for us a far more exceeding *and* eternal weight of glory; while we look not at the things which are seen, but at the things which are not seen: for the things which are seen *are* temporal, but the things which are not seen *are* eternal."

THE
SIXTH DAY

THE SIXTH DAY

Like the third, the sixth day has two parts.

On the third day twice it is written "God saw that it was good," and twice "God said."

On the sixth day we have "God said" *four times*.

Again, it is "living soul" that is brought forth; this time not from the "waters," but from the "earth."

> "Let the earth bring forth the living creature." (Gen. 1:24)

Again, it is "living creature that hath life."

There was life on the fifth day from the waters, there is life on the sixth day from the earth.

And just as the one was *blessing* brought out of the waters of the troubles and sorrows of the flesh *within*, so on the sixth day it is blessing brought forth from the troubles *without*. Joseph is the life-type of this.

He suffered at the hands of man; and those of us who now suffer at the hands of man, suffer because men know not Christ nor the Father.

> "These things will they do unto you, because they have not known the Father, nor Me." (John 16:3)

And this points to the second man, the perfect man, the risen man, to the resurrection of the dead, this life out of the earth – eternal blessing out of the earth. Just as Joseph was the type of the resurrection of the Lord Jesus Christ from the dead, so this true spiritual life which God has implanted in us will not have its consummation until body, soul and spirit know what it is to have the power of this resurrection of Christ manifested in them, and brought forth into the Sabbath-keeping of the seventh day – that rest which has a blessing in it, but which has no morning and no evening. It is …

THE
SEVENTH DAY

THE SEVENTH DAY

Again we have the word "blessed" for the third time, and now at last we have the word "ended."

No more evenings and mornings, but one bright, glorious, eternal day – the sabbath-keeping which remaineth for the people of God (Heb. 4:9).

Now we are able to understand, "in part," what those words mean,

> "If any man *be* in Christ *he* is a new creation: old things are passed away; behold, all things are become NEW." (2 Cor. 5:17)

And to discover the meaning of Ps. 40:5.

> "Many O Lord my God, are Thy wonderful WORKS which thou hast done, and Thy THOUGHTS which are to us-ward: they cannot be reckoned up in order unto Thee: if I would declare and speak of them, they are more than can be numbered."

And as we contemplate the ways of God in creation, and learn from them what He even then purposed to do for lost sinners, we see His ways in Grace and say,

> "Marvellous are Thy WORKS; and that my soul knoweth right well . . . How precious also are Thy THOUGHTS unto me, O God! How great is the sum of them!" (Psa. 139:14-17)

APPENDIX

The following is offered as the STRUCTURE of Gen. 1:2-2:3.

Verse 1. IN THE BEGINNING GOD CREATED THE HEAVENS AND THE EARTH.

A | 2a. The Rest of Chaos.
  B | 2b-5. Light and Darkness. Day and Night (Day 1)
    C | 6-8. The Waters. Division between them. (Day 2)
      D | 9-13. The Earth. Fruit from it. (Day 3)
  B | 14-19. Light holders for the Day and Night. (Day 4)
    C | 20-23. The Waters. Life from them. (Day 5)
      D | 24-31. The Earth. Life from it. (Day 6)
A | 2:1-3. The Rest of Creation. (Day 7)

ALSO ON THIS SUBJECT

ALSO ON THIS SUBJECT

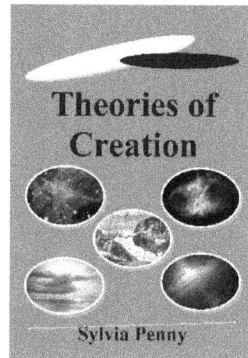

In the Beginning
Beginning
A Study of Genesis 1:1-5
Denis A Wheadon

Theories of Creation
Sylvia Penny

In the Beginning
A Study of Genesis 1:1-5
By Denis A Wheadon

Creation is a fascinating subject and there are many theories about how God created based upon different interpretations of Genesis, and sometimes drawing upon different ideas from science. In this publication the author shares his understanding of creation but not in a dogmatic way.

His view is presented in an objective manner and no space is devoted to negativism towards those who hold different understandings. Rather readers are left to decide for themselves whether they favour this understanding of creation or not.

However, even those who may not agree with his conclusions on *when* and on *how* God created will, none the less, be uplifted by much of what is written, for it all glorifies God as Creator.

****

Theories of Creation
By Sylvia Penny

Creation is a fascinating subject! It is a subject about which there are many theories, in both the Christian and the scientific worlds, but which is the correct one?

In writing the booklet the author outlines a number of the theories put forward by different Christians. Explanation is given as to how each interprets the account of creation as detailed in Genesis chapters 1 and 2. At the end of each explanation the advantages and disadvantages of each one are given dispassionately.

However, the aim of this booklet is to provide information about each theory in an objective manner, so that readers can decide for themselves which theory they favour. If further information is required on a particular theory, then the reader can refer to the bibliography included at the end of this booklet.

****

**These books are available as eBooks
from Amazon Kindle and Apple,
and as KDP paperbacks from Amazon.**

ABOUT THE AUTHOR

Ethelbert W. Bullinger D.D. (1837-1913) was a direct descendant of Heinrich Bullinger, the great Swiss reformer who carried on Zwingli's work after the latter had been killed in war.

E. W. Bullinger was brought up a Methodist but sang in the choir of Canterbury Cathedral in Kent. He trained for and became an Anglican (Episcopalian) minister before becoming Secretary of the Trinitarian Bible Society. He was a man of intense spirituality and made a number of outstanding contributions to biblical scholarship and broad-based evangelical Christianity.

BULLINGER'S LAST BOOK

The Foundations of Dispensational Truth

**Bullinger's last book,
reflecting his mature views.**

This is Bullinger's last book and is his definitive work on the subject of dispensationalism. It covers the ministries of ...

- the prophets,
- the Son of God,
- those that heard Christ, and
- the ministry of Paul, the Apostle to the Gentiles.

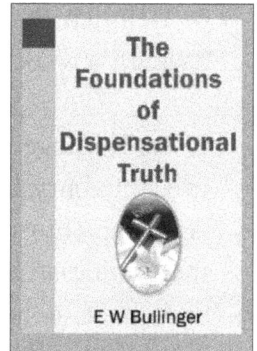

The
Foundations
of
Dispensational
Truth

E W Bullinger

He comments on the Gospels and the Pauline epistles and has a lengthy section on the Acts of the Apostles, followed by one explaining why miraculous signs of the Acts period ceased.

This is a newly typeset book, well presented in an easy to read format.

Copies of *The Foundations of Dispensational Truth,*
and of the books listed on the previous pages
and next pages,
are available from

www.obt.org.uk

and from

The Open Bible Trust,
Fordland Mount, Upper Basildon,
Reading, RG8 8LU, UK.

They also available as eBooks
from Amazon Kindle and Apple,
and as KDP paperbacks from Amazon.

**The following is a selection of works by
E W Bullinger
published by The Open Bible Trust**

The Transfiguration
The Knowledge of God
God's Purpose in Israel
The Prayers of Ephesians
The Lord's Day (Revelation 1:10)
The Rich Man and Lazarus
The Importance of Accuracy
Christ's Prophetic Teaching
The Resurrection of the Body
The Divine Names and Titles
The Spirits in Prison: 1 Peter 3:17-4:6
The Lesson of the Book of Job: The Oldest Lesson in the World
The Seven Sayings to the Woman at the Well
The Foundations of Dispensational Truth
The Christian's Greatest Need
Introducing the Church Epistles
The Two Natures in the Child of God
The Name of Jehovah in the Book of Esther
The Names and Order of the Books of the Old Testament
The Second Advent in Relation to the Jew
The Vision of Isaiah: Its Structure and Scope
The Importance of Accuracy: in the study of the Bible

**More information about the above can be seen
on www.obt.org.uk from where they can be
ordered.**

FURTHER READING

The Development of Dispensationalism

By Michael Penny

This book starts off by considering the theology of four of the earliest church fathers:

- Justin Martyr (110-165)
- Irenaeus (130-200)
- Clement of Alexandria (150-220)
- Augustine (354-430)

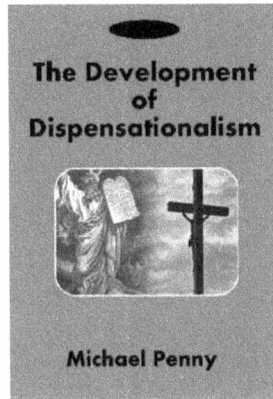

The Development of Dispensationalism

Michael Penny

The author then contrasts their approach to the Bible (which could be termed embryonic dispensationalism) with that of such people as Tertullian (155-222) and Origen (185-254), whose approach was to spiritualize or allegorize.

The healthy debate between two such approaches was cut short by Constantine and the Catholic Church which favoured allegorizing. That was until the reformation when people turned back to the Bible and began to read it and understand it in a more literal way. As a result, Christians, such as Miles Coverdale, began to realise that God had spoken

- at different times, and

- to different people, and
- in different ways.

This is the basis of a dispensational approach and the author does an excellent job is showing how this approach has developed since the Reformation and into the 21st Century.

Search magazine

For a free sample of
the Open Bible Trust's magazine Search,
please email

admin@obt.org.uk

or visit

www.obt.org.uk/search

ABOUT THIS BOOK

THE WAYS OF GOD IN GRACE

Illustrated By

THE WAYS OF GOD IN CREATION

The basis for this book was a Bible Reading given by Dr. E W Bullinger at the Mildmay Conference on the afternoon of Thursday June 23, 1893. He opened the conference with various definitions of 'grace' and concluded that:

> "Grace is the favour of God when there is nothing to draw it forth, nothing to elicit it any way – the uninfluenced favour of God – and in this view creation was at any rate, in a sense, a work of grace."

He then went on to say that there was no reason why God should have created; so far as we know for we are not told. There was no necessity upon His part, for "all things are of God."

He then went on to state that it is just the same in the new creation. The rest of the Bible Reading, and the rest of this book, draws many parallels between the original physical creation recorded in Genesis 1 and 2, and the acts of salvation which results in those who believe in Christ becoming a new creation.

Publications of The Open Bible Trust must be in accordance with its evangelical, fundamental and dispensational basis. However, beyond this minimum, writers are free to express whatever beliefs they may have as their own understanding, provided that the aim in so doing is to further the object of The Open Bible Trust. A copy of the doctrinal basis is available on www.obt.org.uk or from:

THE OPEN BIBLE TRUST
Fordland Mount, Upper Basildon,
Reading, RG8 8LU, UK

.

www.ingramcontent.com/pod-product-compliance
Lightning Source LLC
Chambersburg PA
CBHW060713030426
42337CB00017B/2849